English Code 2

Activity Book

Contents

OUR WORLD

INTRO:
Here we stand: children of every age,
This is our world and the world's our stage.
We can laugh, we can cry — we can float, we can fly,
We can dance, we can sing — we can do almost anything
in OUR world ... our *beautiful* world.

VERSE 1:
Some of us are small; some of us are tall,
Some of us are shy; some say hi to everybody,
Some of us like numbers; some of us love words,
Some of us watch football, and some of us watch the birds!

(CHORUS)
This is *our* world ... we're different but the same.
We live and learn together — we get to know each other ...
in OUR world ... our *beautiful* world.

VERSE 2:
Some of us like music; some of us like cars,
Some of us draw pictures, looking at the stars,
Some of us are scientists, trying to find the code,
All of us can help a friend and give a hand to hold.

This is *our* world — there's room for everyone.
We learn to live together, and we have a lot of fun ...
In **our** world ... in **our** world ... in our beautiful world!

Progress Chart

You did it!

Congratulations!

Unit 8

Unit 7

Unit 6

Unit 5

Unit 4

Unit 3

Unit 2

Unit 1

Creativity

Collaboration

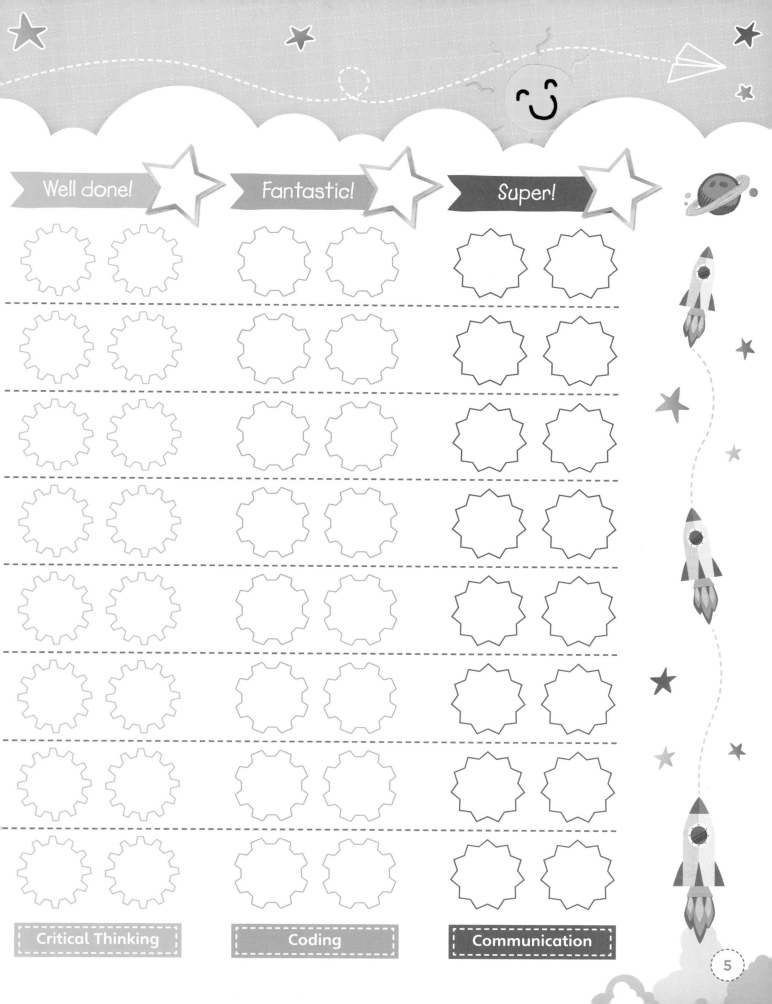

Well done!

Fantastic!

Super!

Critical Thinking

Coding

Communication

Welcome!

 How can I talk about myself?

1 Look, read and match.

1 I climb. _____
2 I swim. _____
3 I draw. _____
4 I sing. _____
5 I read. _____

2 Which day is next? Write.

CODE CRACKER

1 Wednesday, Thursday, _____
2 Saturday, Sunday, _____
3 Thursday, Friday, _____
4 Sunday, Monday, _____
5 Monday, Tuesday, _____
6 Friday, Saturday, _____
7 Tuesday, Wednesday, _____

3 Listen and circle.

Good morning, children / girls and boys !

How are you? It's Thursday / Monday today!

We're at school and we can draw / sing .

And read and write / swim and play!

Months and seasons

VOCABULARY

1 Choose and write the seasons. Then write the months.

autumn   spring
summer   winter

April   August   December   February   January   July
June   March   May   November   October   September

_____   _____   _____   _____

_____   _____   _____   _____

_____   _____   _____   _____

_____   _____   _____   _____

2 Write the months.

MATHS ZONE

1   07   _July_

2   03   _____

3   10   _____

4   02   _____

5   11   _____

6   01   _____

QUIZ!

How many months start with ...

J ? ☐   M ? ☐   A ? ☐

3 Write and draw. Then ask and answer.

My favourite season is

_____ .

What's your favourite season?

Summer!

I can   use months and seasons words.

Language lab 1

GRAMMAR: I'M / I AM

> I will talk about how old I am using **I am ...** / **You are ...** / **He is ...**

1 Write the apostrophe (').

1 I'm

2 Y o u r e

3 H e s

4 S h e s

5 I t s

6 W e r e

7 T h e y r e

2 Read and write.

1 I am eight.   I'm 8.

2 I am seven.   _____

3 You are nine.   _____

4 He is three.   _____

5 She is six.   _____

6 It is ten.   _____

7 We are five.   _____

8 They are two.   _____

3 Listen and write the number. Draw the candles. Then write **am**, **is** or **are**.

1 7

2

I _____ am _____

_____ seven _____ .

You _____

_____ .

3

4

He _____

_____ .

She _____

_____ .

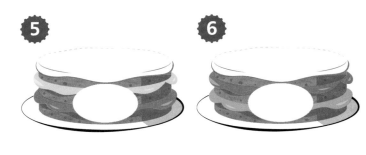

5

6

We _____

_____ .

They _____

_____ .

I can use **I am** / **You are** / **He is**.

Story lab

READING

I will read a story and learn to introduce myself.

Nice to meet you!

1 ✿ Make your story book. ➡ page 115

1 Order and write the page numbers.

2 Complete the story.

3 Draw a cover.

4 Complete the story review.

2 Choose and complete.

are   eight   I'm   name   teacher   your

1 Good morning, children!
My _____ is Miss Kelly.
I'm your _____ .

2 What's _____ name?

_____ Leo!

How old _____ you?

I'm _____ .

3 Circle and match.

- He's / She's Leo.
- He's / She's Anna.
- He's / She's Miss Kelly.
- He's / She's Tom.

1 Out and about!

How can I create a town guide?

1 Look, match and circle.

castle / café

swimming pool / café

castle / swimming pool

2 Circle the odd one out.

CODE CRACKER

1 café

2 swimming pool

3 castle

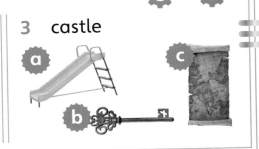

3 Listen to the song. Number the words in order.

school ☐   shops ☐   pool ☐   castle ☐

Where are they?

VOCABULARY

I will learn town words.

1 Label the pictures.

_____ _____ _____ _____

2 Unscramble the words.

1 féac   _____   2 tclase   _____

3 marf   _____   4 suhoe   _____

5 yabrilr   _____   6 usemum   _____

7 kapr   _____   8 unlapydrog   _____

9 erriv   _____   10 coolsh   _____

11 oshp   _____   12 wingsmim loop   _____

_____

EXTRA VOCABULARY

3 🎧 005 Listen, point and say. Then match.

hotel

shopping centre

zoo

a

c

b

I can use town words.

Language lab 1

GRAMMAR 1: LIKE / DON'T LIKE

*I will talk about town words using **like / don't like**.*

1 Look, read and match.

- She doesn't like cafés.

- He likes museums.

- He doesn't like farms.

- She likes school.

2 Circle and write likes or doesn't like.

1 He / She _____ libraries. (Tom)

2 He / She _____ castles. (Monica)

3 He / She _____ shops. (Kate)

4 He / She _____ swimming pools. (Mark)

3 Look, listen and tick ☑.

1 Ben
2 Carla
3 Sam
4 Jenny

a ☺ ☐
b ☹ ☐

a ☺ ☐
b ☹ ☐

a ☺ ☐
b ☹ ☐

a ☺ ☐
b ☹ ☐

4 Read and write . or ? Then circle.

1 Does Ben like school _____   Yes, he does. / No, he doesn't.

2 Carla doesn't like the castle _____   True / False

3 Sam likes the river _____   True / False

4 Does Jenny like the café _____   Yes, she does. / No, she doesn't.

5 Draw 😐 or 🙁 for you. Then choose and write.

Yes, I do.   No, I don't.   like   don't like

Do you like libraries?

_____

I _____ libraries.

Do you like school?

_____

I _____ school.

Do you like shops?

_____

I _____ shops.

6 Make. Then show and tell.

I like cats and cars!

I don't like frogs and pears!

I can   talk about town words using like / don't like .

13

Story lab

READING

I will read a story about a town.

A **special** day

1 Make your story book. → page 117

1 Order and write the page numbers.   2 Complete the story.

3 Draw a cover.   4 Complete the story review.

2 Order and write.

like   castle!   the   I

1 _____

a   We've   cake!   big   got

2 _____

know!   don't   I

3 _____

Town!   birthday,   Happy   Castle

4 _____

3 Choose and colour. Then write and say.

black   blue   brown   green   orange
pink   purple   red   yellow

What colour is your castle?

My castle is
_____ .

4 Read and match.

1 What's happening, Leo?

2 Where are Anna and Leo?

3 Thank you!

You're welcome!

I don't know!

We're here, Miss Kelly!

5 Count and write numbers and words.

MATHS ZONE

How many?

1 red balloons

☐ _____

2 yellow balloons

☐ _____

3 blue balloons

☐ _____

4 white balloons

☐ _____

TOTAL

☐ _____

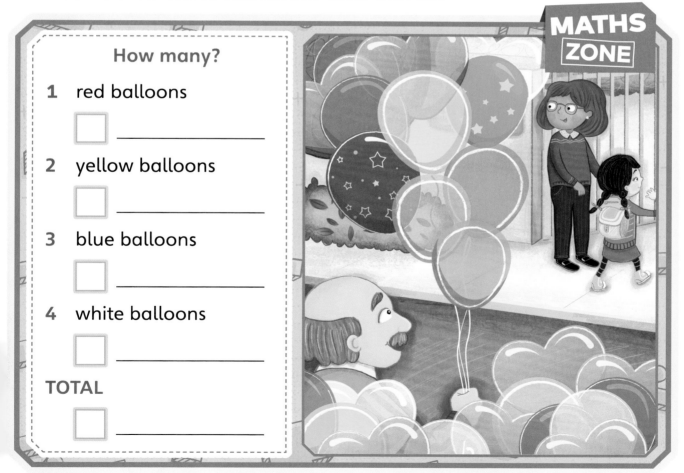

I can read a story about a town.

Phonics lab

I will learn the **a** and **e** sounds.

1 Circle six words.

cappegbagmatwetten

2 Write a or e. Then look and match.

1 c __ p ☐

2 p __ g ☐

3 b __ g ☐

4 m __ t ☐

5 w __ t ☐

6 t __ n ☐

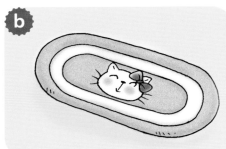

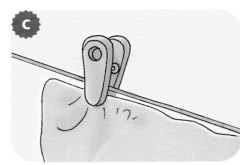

3 Read, listen and circle.

1 mat / wet

2 cap / ten

3 peg / cap

4 mat / peg

5 bag / wet

6 bag / ten

I can use the **a** and **e** sounds.

Experiment lab

ENGINEERING: HOW TO BUILD A HOUSE

I will learn about building materials.

1 Match, choose and write.

bricks   cement   steel   wood

_____ ☐

_____ ☐

_____ ☐

_____ ☐

a

b

c

d

EXPERIMENT TIME

Report

1 Draw a tower.

2 How many bricks do you need? Draw and write.

MATHS ZONE

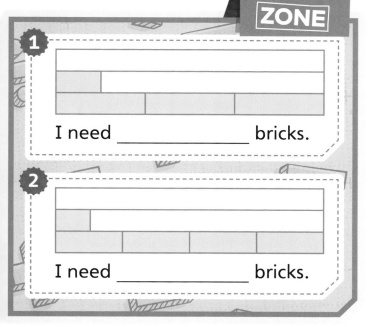

1

I need _____ bricks.

2

I need _____ bricks.

2 Read and circle for you.

My tower is made of cups / clay / spaghetti / card .

My tower is strong / not strong !

I know about building materials.

Language lab 2

GRAMMAR 2: THERE IS / THERE ARE

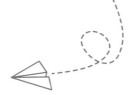

I will describe places using **there is / there are**.

1 Read and draw.

> I like this village! There's a castle! There are three houses and four shops. There's a museum and there are two rivers!

2 Look and say.

> There are 10 shops.

> Picture b!

3 Circle and write about Picture b.

> There's   There are   houses   library

1   **There's** / **There are** a pool.

2   **There's** / **There are** ten shops.

3   **There's** / **There are** a farm.

4   _____ two cafés.

5   There's a _____ .

6   _____ five _____ .

I can use **there is / there are**.

Let's play!

COMMUNICATION

I will talk about games.

1 008 Look, listen and number.

a

☐

b

☐

c
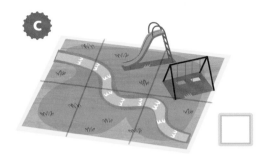
☐

2 Read and match. Then circle game a, b or c.

1
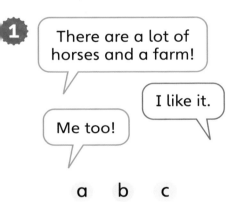

There are a lot of horses and a farm!

I like it.

Me too!

a   b   c

2

It's great! Let's make the castle.

Good idea.

a   b   c

3

Let's play this game. There's a park.

This is my favourite!

Oh, look! There's a river, too.

a   b   c

3 Talk about this game with a partner.

café   castle   farm
house   library
museum   park
playground   river
school   shop
swimming pool

I can talk about games.

Make a town guide

Project report

1 Tick ☑ or cross ☒ and write for your town guide.

	Photo	Drawing	Writing
My school			
My house			
A museum			
A river			
A farm			
_____			

2 Choose, complete and circle for your town.

castle(s)   farm(s)   house(s)   museum(s)   school(s)   shop(s)

1   There's a _____ . I like / don't like the _____ .

2   There's a _____ . I like / don't like the _____ .

3   There are _____ . I like / don't like the _____ .

3 Ask and answer about your partner's favourite place.

What's your favourite place in town?

There is / There are … . I like the … .

I can make a town guide.

4 Look at the photos. Read and tick ☑ T (True) or F (False).

I'm Donny. This is my town.

	T	F
1 There's a farm.	☐	☐
2 There are four houses.	☐	☐
3 There isn't a swimming pool.	☐	☐
4 There are two museums.	☐	☐
5 There aren't any shops.	☐	☐

5  Read, listen and circle.

1 Donny likes / doesn't like the museum.

2 He likes / doesn't like the castle.

3 He likes / doesn't like the cafés.

6 Now talk to a partner about Donny's town.

Do you like the museum?

Now go to your Progress Chart on page 4.

2 Day and night

How can I talk about day and night?

1 Look, read and write a or b.

It's day.   It's night.

1   There's a porcupine and it's dark.   _____

2   There's a donkey and it's light.   _____

3   There's an owl, a bat and a fox.   _____

2 Read and colour.

CODE CRACKER

1

Look at the owl. It's night. The sky is black. The Moon is white.

2

Look at the donkey. It's day. The sky is blue. The Sun is yellow.

3 Read and circle. Then listen and order.

a   At night, at night, the owl / I wakes up.

b   In the day, in the day, I sleep / wake up .

c   At night, at night, I sleep / wake up .

d   In the day, in the day, he sleep / sleeps .

What is it?

VOCABULARY

I will learn animal and daily routine words.

CODE CRACKER

1 **What comes next? Circle the picture and write.**

1 cow donkey cow donkey

 _____

2 bat owl owl bat

 _____

3 goat goat porcupine goat

 _____

4 bat bat cow cow

 _____

5 porcupine porcupine donkey donkey

 _____

6 donkey donkey goat donkey

 _____

EXTRA VOCABULARY

2 **Listen and say. Then match.** 011

deer

snake

wolf

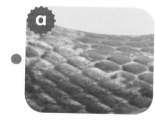
a

b

c

I can use animal and daily routine words.

23

Language lab 1

GRAMMAR 1: I GO / DON'T GO

I will talk about daily routines.

1 Circle, choose and complete.

brush   go   go   wake

1   I / We _____ to school.

2   I / We _____ to school.

3   I / We _____ our teeth.

4   I / We _____ up.

2 Order for you.

brush my teeth   eat   go to school   sleep   wake up   wash my face

3 Listen and circle.

1   Do you wash your hands at school?   Yes, I do. / No, I don't.

2   Do you eat at school?   Yes, I do. / No, I don't.

3   Do you brush your teeth at school?   Yes, I do. / No, I don't.

4   Do you sleep at school?   Yes, I do. / No, I don't.

4 Complete for you.

1 wake up   I _____don't wake up_____ in the playground.

2 sleep   I _____ in the library.

3 eat   I _____ at home.

4 wash my hands   I _____ at the café.

5 brush my teeth   I _____ in the swimming pool.

5 Read and tick ☑ T (True) or F (False). Then say.

	T	F
1 Cows eat pizza.	☐	☐
2 Bats sleep in the day.	☐	☐
3 Porcupines go to school.	☐	☐
4 Goats brush their teeth.	☐	☐
5 Donkeys eat grass.	☐	☐
6 Owls wash their hands.	☐	☐

Cows don't eat pizza!

6 Make cards and play the *Do you …?* game.

Do you eat in the swimming pool?

No, I don't!

I can talk about daily routines.

Story lab

READING

I will read a story about farm animals.

Do goats dance?

1 ⚙ **Make your story book.** ➡ **page 119**

1 Order and write the page numbers.

2 Complete the story.

3 Draw a cover.

4 Complete the story review.

2 Read and match.

1 Do cows sing?

2 Do goats dance, Miss Kelly?

3 Hello, Mrs Hay. What's happening?

● I don't know.

● No, Tom! They don't sing. They say 'moo!'

● No, Tom! They don't dance!

3 Join the dots. Then choose and complete.

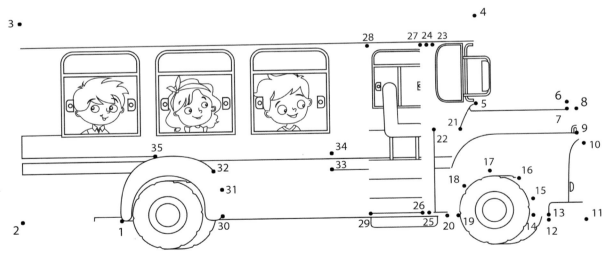

at Mrs Hay's farm   at school   on the bus

Anna, Leo and Tom are _____ .

4 Order and write.

1 music   !   They   the   like

_____

2 is   cow   .   a   This

_____

5 Find, count and write.

1 There are _____ cows.

2 There are _____ sheep.

3 There are _____ donkeys.

4 There are _____ goats.

5 There are _____ animals.

6 Now do the maths.

MATHS ZONE

1 How many cows' legs are there on the farm? ☐

2 How many sheep's legs are there on the farm? ☐

3 How many goats' legs are there on the farm? ☐

7 What happens next?
Tick ☑ and draw your idea.

The animals go to school. ☐

The animals sleep. ☐

The animals eat grass. ☐

I can read a story about farm animals.

I will learn the **i** and **o** sounds.

1 Circle and write the words with the **i** sound.

 	British		American
	bin		trash can

h	a	t	o	b	e	k
i	c	p	d	n	l	p
t	r	b	i	n	v	g
s	i	x	g	i	m	z
w	g	n	o	s	u	i
r	t	y	j	x	h	q

_____ _____

_____ _____

2 Write **o** and match.

1 j_____g •

2 f_____x •

3 h_____t •

•   •   •

3 🎧 013 Read, listen and write **i** or **o**.

1 S_____x l_____ttle ch_____ldren s_____t and s_____ng.

2 St_____p the fr_____g!

I can use the **i** and **o** sounds.

Experiment lab

I will learn about the Earth and the Sun.

1 Label the picture.

day   Earth   night   Sun

1 _____

2 _____

3 _____

4 _____

2 Look, read and match.

1 24 hours •   • 1 year •

2 12 months •   • 1 day •

EXPERIMENT TIME

Report

1 Write your report. Tick ☑ the correct picture and complete the sentence.

Earth   Sun

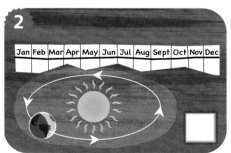

The _____
       goes around the
_____ .

I know about the Earth and the Sun.

Language lab 2

GRAMMAR 2: SHE EATS / DOESN'T EAT

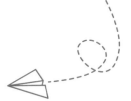
I will ask and answer about daily routines.

1 Look and say.

It's Saturday! What do they do?

 My name is Megan.

 She eats an apple.

 My name is Danny.

 He goes to the museum.

2 Choose and write answers.

No, he doesn't.   No, she doesn't.   Yes, he does.   Yes, she does.

1   Does Megan go to school on Saturday?   _____

2   Does she brush her teeth?   _____

3   Does Danny go to the library on Saturday?   _____

4   Does he wash his hands?   _____

3 Circle and write about Megan or Danny.

eats   doesn't eat   doesn't go   goes

It's Saturday! He / She _____ to school.

He / She _____ to the museum / library .

He / She _____ an apple / a banana .

- -

30 **I can** ask and answer about daily routines.

What time is it?

COMMUNICATION

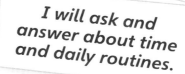

I will ask and answer about time and daily routines.

1 🎧 014 **Listen and circle. Then match.**

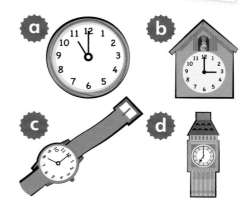

a   b   c   d

1   It's **seven** / **five** o'clock. ☐

2   It's **twelve** / **three** o'clock. ☐

3   It's **four** / **eleven** o'clock. ☐

4   It's **eight** / **ten** o'clock. ☐

2 💬 **What time do you wake up? Talk to a partner.**

I wake up at seven o'clock on Monday.

3 💬 **Ask and answer with a partner. Then circle *Yes* or *No*.**

My friend			
_____			Yes / No
_____			Yes / No
_____			Yes / No

Do you wake up at six o'clock on Saturday?

No, I don't. I wake up at seven o'clock.

4 💬 **Now tell the class.**

Do a day and night presentation

Project report

1 Tick ☑ or cross ☒ for your presentation.

	I have pictures of ...	I talk about ...	I write about ...
The Sun			
The Moon			
Animals			
Me			
A friend			
My school			
_____			

2 Draw, choose and write.

wake up / sleep / eat   wakes up / sleeps / eats

1 ● In the day, I _____ .

   ☾ At night, I _____ .

2

   ● It _____ .

   ☾ It _____ .

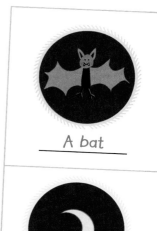

A bat

It sleeps.

I can do a day and night presentation.

3 Write one thing you say in your presentation.

_____

_____

4 Look, read and circle T (True) or F (False).

1 I wake up at six o'clock.   T / F

2 I eat an orange every day.   T / F

3 I don't brush my teeth at night.   T / F

4 I go to school at nine o'clock.   T / F

I'm Ken.

5 015 Look, listen and circle.

1 Stella wakes up at

a   b

2 She eats

a    b

3 She goes to school at

a    b

This is my friend, Stella.

6 Now talk to a partner about Ken and Stella.

Does Ken wake up at five o'clock?

No, he doesn't.

Now go to your Progress Chart on page 4.

1 Checkpoint

UNITS 1 AND 2

1. Complete the table.

bat   brush my teeth   cow   donkey   go to school   goat
library   museum   park   playground   sleep   wash my face

Town	Animals	Things I do
_____ _____	_____ _____	_____ _____
_____ _____	_____ _____	_____ _____

2. Draw a path.

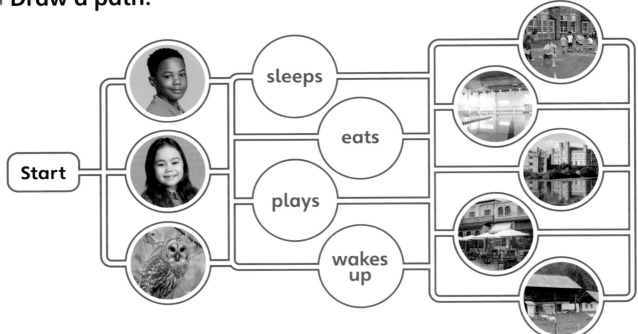

3. Look at 2. Write, then ask and answer with a partner.

1   Who is it? _____

2   What does he / she / it do? _____

3   Where? _____

Long nights, long days

1 Read, complete and match.

Antarctica   Arctic   bears   seals

1 This is a town in the _____ . ☐

2 There are elks and _____ ! ☐

3 This man is in _____ . ☐

4 There are elephant _____ . ☐

2 Circle, draw and colour.

3 Write about you and the animals in your country.

The Arctic

It's December / June . The sky is black. The Moon is in the sky all day and all night.

My name is _____ .

I live in _____ .

There are _____ in my country.

Antarctica

It's December / June . The sky is blue. The Sun is in the sky all day and all night.

3 Lost and found

How can I make a class museum?

1 Count and answer the questions.

MATHS ZONE

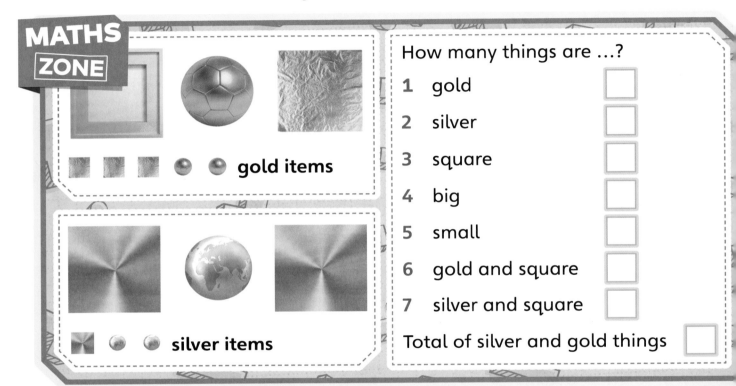

gold items

silver items

How many things are ...?

1 gold ☐

2 silver ☐

3 square ☐

4 big ☐

5 small ☐

6 gold and square ☐

7 silver and square ☐

Total of silver and gold things ☐

2 Draw and colour. Then circle and write.

gold   silver   square

1 It's a (house) / book . It's _____ .

CODE CRACKER

2 It's (an apple) / a ball . It's _____ .

3 It's a (cat) / bird . It's _____ .

What does it look like?

I will learn words to describe things.

1 Look, choose and write.

clean	dirty
gold	hard
heavy	light
new	old
round	silver
soft	square

1 _____ 2 _____ 3 _____ 4 _____

5 _____ 6 _____ 7 _____ 8 _____

9 _____ 10 _____ 11 _____ 12 _____

EXTRA VOCABULARY

2 Look, listen and say.

016

1 shiny 2 colourful 3 broken

3 Now point and say.

It's …

I can use words to describe things.

Language lab 1

GRAMMAR 1: MINE / YOURS / HIS / HERS

I will ask and answer about objects using **mine / yours / his / hers**.

1 Read, circle and match.

1 It's a doll. It's for you. It's mine / yours .

2 It's a teddy bear. It's for me. It's mine / yours .

3 It's an aeroplane. It's for Ben. It's his / hers .

4 It's a boat. It's for Sally. It's his / hers .

2 017 Look, listen and match.

3 Read, draw and colour.

Simon

Bella

CODE CRACKER

Simon and Bella have new clothes.

The yellow T-shirt is his.

The red T-shirt is hers.

The blue trousers are his.

The green trousers are hers.

The purple shoes are his.

The black shoes are hers.

4 Find and write.

It's his.   It's hers.

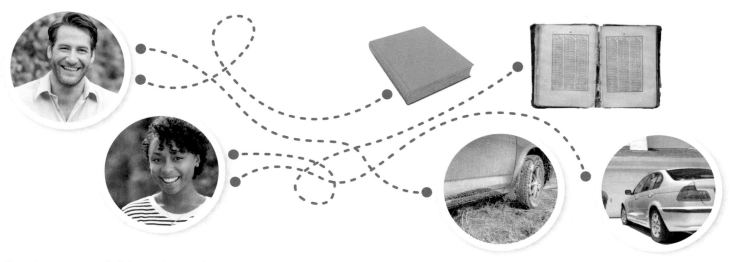

1 It's an old book. Whose is it? _____

2 It's a new book. Whose is it? _____

3 It's a dirty car. Whose is it? _____

4 It's a clean car. Whose is it? _____

5 Choose and tick ☑ three pets for you and cross ☒ three pets for your partner.

6 🗨 Talk to your partner.

Whose is the cat?

The cat is mine. The hamster is yours.

7 Now write *my* or *your*.

1 It's _____ cat.

2 It's _____ hamster.

3 It's _____ fish.

4 It's _____ frog.

5 It's _____ rabbit.

6 It's _____ bird.

Story lab

> *I will read a story about something Anna finds.*

1 ⚙ Make your story book. ➡ page 121

1 Order and write the page numbers.
2 Complete the story.
3 Draw a cover.
4 Complete the story review.

2 Order and write. Then read and match.

1 time, Mud ? Mr the What's

_____ ☐

2 ? it like What look does

_____ ☐

3 his his ! ! It's It's

_____ ☐

a Yes, it's mine.

b Two o'clock …
no … three … no …

c It's square. It's
dirty. It's made
of wood.

3 Look and tick ☑. Then say.

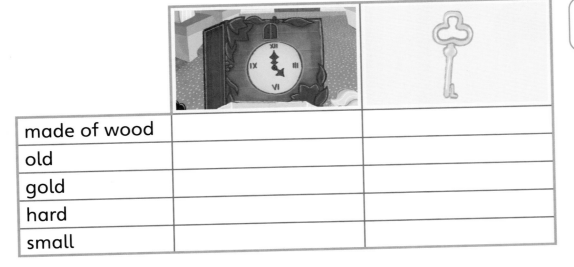

made of wood		
old		
gold		
hard		
small		

> The cuckoo clock
> is made of wood.

4 Read and tick ☑ T (True) or F (False).

T F

1   There are tomato plants in the garden.

2   The cuckoo clock is round.

3   The key is small and silver.

4   Mr Mud is happy with the cuckoo clock.

5 🗨 Ask and answer with a partner. Point at the correct key.

Look! It's a key!

What does it look like?

It's small and silver.

6 ✷ Make a cuckoo clock. Then talk about your clock.

Whose clock is this?

It's mine!

GLUE

Phonics lab

I will learn the **u** and **x** sounds.

1 Look and write u or x. Then listen and number.

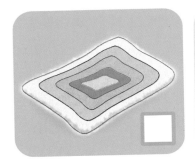

r____g

fo____

s____n

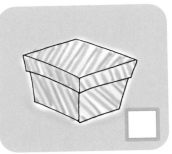

bo____

n____t

r____n

si____

ta____i

2 What's next? Read and circle.

CODE CRACKER

1 bug six rug taxi   run / ox

2 ox box sun fox   taxi / nut

3 jug nut ox run   box / sun

3 Circle the correct letters.

1   g x I
    b u

2   u x f
    o r

3   t n u
    j g

 I can use the **u** and **x** sounds.

Experiment lab

SCIENCE: SOLIDS AND LIQUIDS

I will learn about solids and liquids.

1 Write L for liquid or S for solid. Then match.

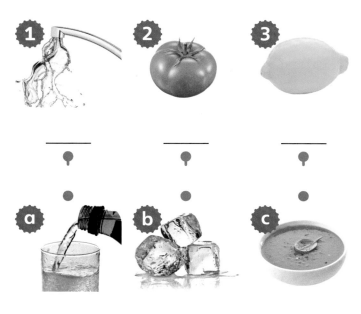

1 _____   **2** _____   **3** _____

a _____   **b** _____   **c** _____

2 Now point and say.

This is a liquid. Now it's a solid!

3 Now read and circle T (True) or F (False).

1   Liquids have no shape.   T / F

2   Solids are always round.   T / F

3   Liquids are hard.   T / F

4   Solids are sometimes soft.   T / F

5   Solids and liquids sometimes change.   T / F

EXPERIMENT TIME

Report

1 Write 1–3 in order. Then choose and write.

cornflour   jug   liquid   solid

a   This is a _____.

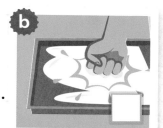

b

This is a _____.

c   A _____ of water.

_____

2 Now tick ☑ for you.

My liquid changes. ☐

My liquid doesn't change. ☐

I know about solids and liquids.

Language lab 2

GRAMMAR 2: OUR / OURS   THEIR / THEIRS

I will ask about objects using **ours / theirs**.

1 Write your names. Then colour the toys.

Me: _____

My partner: _____

blue   green   orange   purple   red   yellow

2 Now show and tell.

What colour is your owl?

Our owl is …

3 Look, choose and write.

blue   green   orange   purple   red   yellow

Leo and Anna have got the same toys!

Their owl is _____ . Ours is _____ .

Our car is _____ . Theirs is _____ .

Their train is _____ . _____ is _____ .

Our horse is _____ . _____ is _____ .

I can ask about objects using ours and theirs .

A fun scavenger hunt!

COMMUNICATION

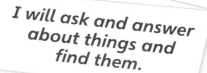

I will ask and answer about things and find them.

1 Listen and match. Write 1–6.

1  **2**  **3**  **4**  **5**  **6**

 Mark ☐ ☐ ☐

 Tina ☐ ☐ ☐

2 Look at 1. Ask and answer with a partner.

Whose toy is this? The soft toy? Yes. It's his.

3 Point and talk about these things with a partner.

> It's hers.   It's his.   It's mine.
> It's ours.   It's theirs.   It's yours.

book   desk   pencil case   rubber   ruler   school

Whose desk is this?

Whose rubber is this?

It's theirs!

It's ours!

Create a class museum

Project report

1 Tick ☑ or cross ☒ .

In our museum, there are …

	old	new	big	small
photos				
books				
rocks				
dolls				
cars				
toys				
_____				

2 Read and circle for your museum.

1 There is / isn't an old toy.

2 There is / isn't a beautiful rock.

3 There is / isn't a black and white photo.

4 There is / isn't a big book.

3 What is your favourite thing in your museum? Draw and write.

This is a teddy bear.
It's soft and old. It's beautiful!

This is a _____ .

It's _____ .

I can create a class museum.

4 Look and read. Then tick ☑ or cross ☒.

1

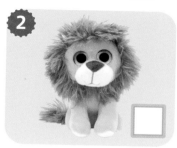
2

3

4

This is an old car.　　This is a soft toy.　　This is a round ball.　　This is dirty water.

5 Read and complete.

old　round　silver

I'm Tania and this is my brother, Peter.

Look at our museum. It's the Museum of Beautiful Things!

I've got a pen. It's _____ and gold.

Peter's got an owl. It's old and _____ .

Peter and I have got a lot of marbles. They're hard and _____ .

6 Now choose and write.

1　The pen is _____ .

2　The owl is _____ .

3　The marbles are _____ .

his
theirs
hers

Now go to your Progress Chart on page 4.

4 At the gallery

How can I create a portrait gallery?

1 Circle a, b or c. Then point and say.

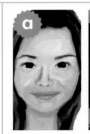        

1 happy   sad   angry   a   b   c

2 angry   sad   happy   a   b   c

3 happy   angry   sad   a   b   c

2 Think. Then choose for you and say.

angry   happy   sad

I look at this picture and I am …

3 Listen to the song and order.

shy ☐   happy ☐   kind ☐   angry ☐

I am happy!

VOCABULARY

I will learn describing words for people and pets.

1 Look, read and number.

1 angry   2 friendly   3 happy   4 helpful   5 kind   6 sad

2 Read, colour and write the names.

CODE CRACKER

Tina's got a red T-shirt. She's funny!

Maria's got a yellow T-shirt. She's shy.

Billy's got a blue T-shirt. He's tired.

EXTRA VOCABULARY

3 Listen and say. Then match.

sporty ●   ● Good morning. How are you today?

chatty ●   ● Hi! Hello! Do you like English? Me too! Let's talk!

polite ●   ● I can climb!

I can use words for describing people and pets.

Language lab 1

*I will describe people using **always** / **sometimes** / **never**.*

1 Follow and order the jumbled letters for each person. Then write He's or She's.

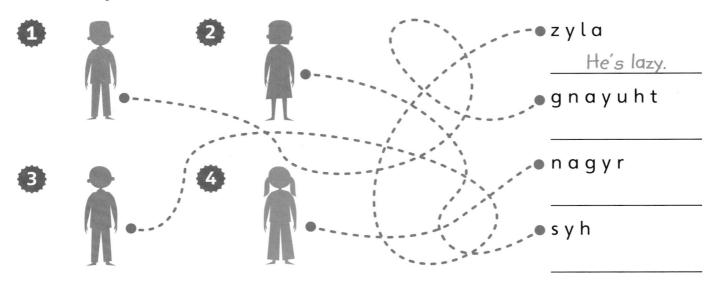

z y l a

_____He's lazy._____

g n a y u h t

_____

n a g y r

_____

s y h

_____

2 Look, read and write.

No, he isn't.   No, she isn't.   Yes, he is.   Yes, she is.

1 Is he young?   _____

2 Is he friendly?   _____

3 Is she helpful?   _____

4 Is she old?   _____

3 Look and write He is or He isn't.

1 _____ friendly.

2 _____ angry.

3 _____ kind.

4 _____ naughty.

4 Circle, choose and write.

1   He / She is

_____ funny.

2   He / She is

_____ helpful.

3   He / She is

_____ sad.

5 Make a word picture. Draw and write about a friend or someone in your family.

6 Now show and tell.

This is my brother. He's sometimes naughty! He's always funny.

HAPPY FRIENDLY NAUGHTY FUN NAUGHTY FUNNY HAPPY FRIENDLY

THIS IS MY   BROTHER

I can use always / sometimes / never.

51

Story lab

READING

I will read a story about a painting competition.

Who is this?

1 ✺ Make your story book. ➡ page 123

1 Order and write the page numbers.
2 Complete the story.
3 Draw a cover.
4 Complete the story review.

2 Look, read and match.

1 Who is this, Tom?

2 Who is this, Mrs Hay?

3 The gold cup goes to … Mr Mud!

Congratulations, Mr Mud!

It's my friend.

It's my cousin. He's sometimes naughty and always happy!

3 Choose, complete and match.

crayons   paints   pencils   photo

 1 I've got a _____ !

 2 I've got _____ and _____ .

 3 I've got my _____ .

a
b
c

52

4 Tick ☑ T (True) or F (False).

		T	F
1	Mrs Hay paints her friend.	☐	☐
2	Tom paints his brother.	☐	☐
3	Mr Mud paints Milly.	☐	☐
4	Milly paints Mr Mud.	☐	☐

5 Work with a partner. Point, ask and answer.

Who is this?

It's Anna. That's her nose.

6 What happens next? Choose, tick ☑ and draw.

1 ☐ Milly is tired now!

2 ☐ Milly's got the gold cup now!

3 ☐ Look! What a lovely rainbow!

I will learn the j and y sounds.

1 Write j or y and match.

1 _____ump

2 _____es

3 _____o-_____o

4 _____uice

5 _____oung

6 _____eans

7 _____ungle

8 _____ellow

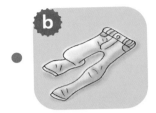

2 🎧 022 Listen and circle.

1 jaguar / yoghurt

2 yak / jar

3 yours / jeans

4 yellow / jungle

3 Write j or y and draw.

There's a _____aguar in the _____ungle! It's _____ellow and black.

I can use the j and y sounds.

Experiment lab

ART AND DESIGN: CHANGING FACES

I will learn about changing faces.

1 Label the face.

eyebrow   eye colour   lines   smile

1 _____   2 _____

3 _____   4 _____

2 💡 Read and circle.

 a

 b

1 She looks angry.   a / b

2 Her eyes look big.   a / b

3 Her mouth looks big.   a / b

3 💬 Now talk to a partner.

Her eyes look small.

Picture b!

EXPERIMENT TIME

Report

1 Look, read and match.

 1

 2

 3

cry   laugh   yawn

2 Now write for you.

always   never   sometimes

In our experiment …

My partner laughs.
I _____ laugh.

My partner yawns.
I _____ yawn.

My partner cries.
I _____ cry.

I know about changing faces.

Language lab 2

GRAMMAR 2: HAVE YOU GOT ...?

I will ask and answer about people and objects using **have got**.

1 Read, do the maths and colour.

MATHS ZONE

Have you got a dog? ☐

dog: nose = 15 + 2, body = 18 − 6

Have you got a mouse? ☐

mouse: nose = 12 + 7, body = 3 x 3

Have you got a cat? ☐

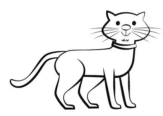

cat: nose = 20 − 3, body = 2 x 7

Have you got a rabbit? ☐

rabbit: nose = 20 − 1, body = 8 + 1

9 = grey   12 = brown   14 = orange   17 = black   19 = pink

2 💬 Now tick ☑ two animals from **1**. Then ask and answer with a partner.

> Have you got a rabbit?

> No, I haven't. / Yes, I have.

> What colour is its nose?

> It's ...

> What colour is its body?

56

I can ask and answer using have got .

Let's take a photo!

COMMUNICATION

I will talk about funny photos.

1 **Look, listen and tick ☑.**

1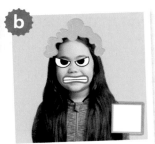

2

2 💬 **Listen again and circle the sentences you hear. Role-play with a partner.**

1   Let's take a photo! / Let's do a photo!

2   Okay … I can wait … I can look! / Okay … wait … look!

3   Oh, this is funny photo. / Oh, that's a funny photo.

3 💬 **Choose a picture. Draw your face. Then talk to a partner.**

Look at me!

Have you got a hat?

Yes, I have!

Are you happy?

I can talk about funny photos.

1 Write and tick ☑ or cross ☒ for your gallery.

	Name	Painting	Drawing	Photo
Friend				
Family				
Teacher				
Pet				
_____				

2 Read and complete. Then tick ☑ the questions you ask.

Are favourite got old sometimes

1 How _____ are you? ☐

2 What's your _____ day? ☐

3 _____ you happy today? ☐

4 Are you _____ sad? ☐

5 Have you _____ a pet? ☐

3 Draw and write about a friend's picture.

This picture is by Ava.
It's her mum.
She's always happy.

This picture is by

_____ .

It's

_____ .

I can create a portrait gallery.

4 Read and tick ☑ the correct sentences.

1

a This is my friend. He isn't happy.
He's sad. ☐

b This is my friend. He isn't sad.
He's happy. ☐

c This is my friend. She isn't sad.
She's happy. ☐

2

a This is my cousin. She isn't tired.
She's angry. ☐

b This is my cousin. He isn't angry.
He's tired. ☐

c This is my cousin. She isn't angry.
She's tired. ☐

5 🎧 Listen and circle.

1 Have you got a pet?   Yes, I have. / No, I haven't.

2 What's its name?   Lulu / Pepper

3 Are you sometimes shy?   Yes, I am. / No, I'm not.

4 What's your favourite colour?   blue / purple

6 💬 Now work with a partner. Ask and answer for you.

Now go to your Progress Chart on page 4.

2 Checkpoint

UNITS 3 AND 4

1 Circle the odd one out.

1 clean   dirty   tomato   heavy   light

2 happy   theirs   friendly   kind   helpful

3 round   his   hers   ours   yours

2 Draw a path.

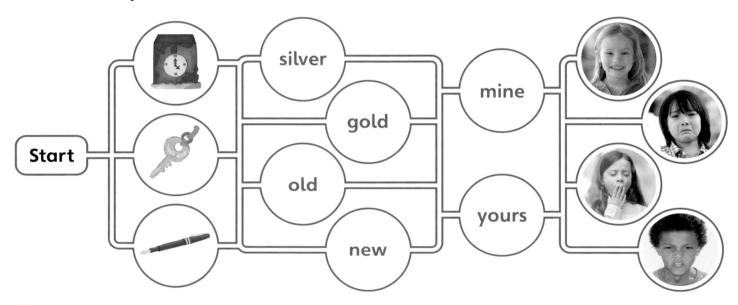

Start

silver
gold
old
new
mine
yours

3 Look at 2. Write your answers and draw.

1 What have you got?

_____

2 What does it look like?

It's _____ .

Music around the world

1 Choose and write.

bagpipes   drum   pipes   sticks   strings   veena

1

2

3

_____

_____

_____

_____

_____

_____

2 Read and circle.

1   The drums are square /
    round .

2   The drums are heavy / light .

3   The bagpipes have got a soft
    / hard bag.

4   The pipes are short / long .

5   The veena is small / big .

6   The veena is square / round .

3 Draw a musical instrument from your country. Then write and circle.

This is a _____ .

It's _____ and _____ .

I like / don't like this instrument.

The music makes me feel happy /
sad / angry / tired .

5 Come in!

How can I create a class meal?

1 Look, read and write a, b or c.

1 I've got pasta. I haven't got biscuits. ☐

2 I've got biscuits. I haven't got pasta. ☐

3 I've got pasta. I haven't got cheese. ☐

2 Look, choose and write.

CODE CRACKER

Come in!
Goodbye!
Thank you!

_____   _____   _____

3 🎧 025 Listen to the song. Order. Write 1–4.

a Would you like some cheese? ☐

b Yes, please! ☐

c Would you like some biscuits? ☐

d We're happy that you're here. ☐

Do you like biscuits?

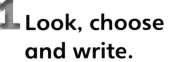 *I will learn food words.*

1 Look, choose and write.

> biscuits   bread   cheese   chicken   fish   ice cream
> juice   pasta   rice   salad   soup   water

1 _____

2 _____

3 _____

4 _____

5 _____

6 _____

7 _____

8 _____

9 _____

10 _____

11 _____

12 _____

EXTRA VOCABULARY

2 026 Listen and say. Then match.

1 cucumber

2 carrot

3 peas

a

b

c

I can use food words.

63

Language lab 1

GRAMMAR 1: CAN I HAVE ...?

I will ask for things politely using Can I have ...?

1 Follow, circle and write Can I have some ..., please?

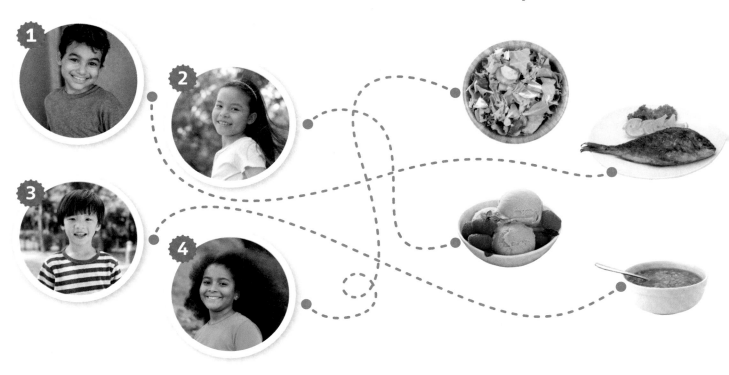

1 _____ fish / salad , _____ ?

2 _____ soup / ice cream , _____ ?

3 _____ salad / soup , _____ ?

4 _____ salad / ice cream , _____ ?

2 🎧 027 Listen, number and circle.

a

b

c

d

Of course! /
Sorry, no.

Of course! /
Sorry, no.

Of course! /
Sorry, no.

Of course! /
Sorry, no.

3 Read and do the maths. Then read and write Of course! or Sorry, no.

MATHS ZONE

ICE CREAM £4

£3   £3

£6   £7   £8

£1   £5   £4

1 Can I have pasta, bread and juice?   Total: £ _____

2 Can I have soup, chicken and salad?   Total: £ _____

3 Can I have ice cream and biscuits? Total: £ _____

4 I've got 10 pounds. Can I have fish and bread?   _____

5 I've got 10 pounds. Can I have pasta and two ice creams? _____

6 I've got 5 pounds. Can I have biscuits and bread?   _____

7 I've got 5 pounds. Can I have chicken and pasta?   _____

4 Play the *Can I have ...?* game with a partner.

| PASTA | CHEESE | FISH |
| SALAD | SOUP | CHICKEN |

5 Now play the *Spell and Ask* game with a partner.

Can I have c-h-i-c-k-e-n, please?

Sorry, no.

Can I have f-i-s-h, please?

Of course!

I can ask for things politely using Can I have ...?

Story lab

I will read a story about Tom's cousin.

Come over and play!

1 **Look, choose and complete.**

Come   cousin   Grandma   here

Can   course   have   please   some

1

Tom, look! _____ and Aunt Julia are _____ ! And your _____ , Adam!

_____ in!

2

Can I _____ some water, _____ ?

_____ I have _____ juice, please?

Yes, of _____ !

Can   okay   this

book   dear   okay   sorry

3

_____ I have _____ car?

Er ... _____ .

4

Oh _____ ! I'm _____ , Tor

Can I have this _____ ?

Er ... _____ .

2 Circle T (True) or F (False).

1   It's Sunday.   T / F

2   Grandma, Aunt Julia and Adam are at school.   T / F

3   Tom's got a lot of toys.   T / F

4   The book is for Adam. It's his book.   T / F

5   Adam and Tom make a cake.   T / F

3 Read and tick ☑ or cross ☒.

It's seven o'clock.

This is Tom's cousin.

This is Grandma.

Tom is happy.

4 💡 Circle the odd one out.

1   cousin   aunt   cake

2   car   school   train

3   water   book   juice

4   Saturday   Adam   Julia

5 💬 What do you think? Tick ☑ and say.

	old	young	kind	funny	naughty
Adam is					
Grandma is					
Tom is					
Mum is					

6 What happens next? ➡ page 125

I can read a story about Tom's cousin.

Phonics lab

I will learn the **ch** and **sh** sounds.

1 Write ch. Then point and say.

1 _____ips   2 _____ocolate

3 _____erries   4 _____eese

2 Circle and say the words with the sh sound. Then write.

s	a	r	x	i	n	c	h
h	d	s	h	i	r	t	e
i	j	e	g	d	z	f	c
p	t	x	a	c	y	s	w
q	u	r	k	u	b	h	q
s	h	e	l	f	v	o	l
c	b	m	w	o	i	p	d
j	e	t	h	f	a	k	g
x	s	h	o	e	s	n	p
d	y	l	u	b	o	r	h
t	s	m	s	h	e	e	p

1 _____

2 _____

3 _____

4 _____

5 _____

6 _____

3 Read and write sh or ch. Then listen and circle.

1 _____orts   _____oes   2 _____air   _____ess

3 _____icken   _____eese   4 _____irt   _____eep

I can use the **ch** and **sh** sounds.

Experiment lab

TECHNOLOGY: MILK

1 Choose and write.

almonds   coconuts   cows   goats
horses   sheep   soya beans

Animals	Plants

2 Look and circle. Then read and tick ☑ T (True) or F (False).

This is a factory / shop .

This is a farmer / combine harvester .

	T	F
1 We always get milk from animals.	☐	☐
2 We sometimes get milk from plants.	☐	☐
3 Farmers sometimes use combine harvesters.	☐	☐
4 Shops make milk clean and healthy.	☐	☐

EXPERIMENT TIME

Report

1 Circle, choose and write.

chocolate   ice   milk   salt
strawberry   sugar   vanilla

In my ice cream there is
_____ from an animal / a plant .

There is _____ and
_____ .

There isn't any _____ .

2 Tick ☑ for you.

I can make ice cream.	☐
I can't make ice cream.	☐
My ice cream is very good!	☐
My ice cream is not very good.	☐

 about making milk.

Language lab 2

GRAMMAR 2: CAN I HAVE THIS / THAT ...?

1 Choose and write This ... or That ... .

ice cream
juice   salad

 **1**

 **2**

 **3**

This salad _____   _____   _____

_____   _____   _____

 **4**

 **5**

 **6**

_____   _____   _____

_____   _____   _____

2 Draw and colour. Then write.

blue   green   orange   pink   purple   red   yellow

Draw a robot on the table. Draw a robot on the shelf.
Draw a ball on the table. Draw a ball on the shelf.

1 This robot is _____ .

2 _____ robot is _____ .

3 _____ ball is _____ .

4 _____ ball is _____ .

I can ask and answer using this / that .

Let's order some food!

I will ask and answer about food.

1 🎧 029 **Listen and tick ☑.**

1 **a** **b**
2 **a** **b**

3 **a** **b**

2 💬 **Look at 1. Ask and answer with a partner.**

Can I have fish and pasta, please?

Thank you.

Can I have ice cream?

Sorry, no.

Of course!

3 💬 **Ask and answer with a partner. Tick ☑ or cross ☒. Then draw.**

Would you like cheese?

Yes, please. / No, thank you.

cheese	☐	soup	☐
juice	☐	biscuits	☐
water	☐	ice cream	☐

My partner would like …

I can ask and answer about food.

PROJECT AND REVIEW UNIT 5

Create a class meal

Project report

1 Tick ☑ or cross ☒ and write in the table about your class meal.

We've got ...	We draw the food	We make the food
chicken		
bread		
salad		
water		

2 Colour the table for your class. Then write.

MATHS ZONE

Number of children

	0	5	10	15	20	25

In my class ...

_____ children like cheese.

_____ children like fish.

_____ children like ice cream.

_____ children like biscuits.

3 Draw your class meal and write.

This is our class meal.

We like _____ .

We don't like _____ .

I can create a class meal.

4 Look, read and match.

 a    b    c    d   e    f

1
Can I have some cheese and salad, please?

Yes, of course. Here you are.

Can I have some juice?

Would you like orange juice or tomato juice?

Orange juice, please.

☐ ☐ ☐

2
Can I have some chicken and pasta, please?

Of course.

Can I have some juice?

Would you like orange juice or tomato juice?

Tomato juice, please.

☐ ☐ ☐

5 Read and colour.

This soup is yellow. That soup is red.

That ice cream is green. This ice cream is pink.

This bread is brown. That bread is white.

1    **2**

3    **4**

6 Colour the juice. Now point and say.

Can I have some juice, please?

This juice or that juice?

That juice. The green juice!

5    **6**

7    **8**

Now go to your Progress Chart on page 4.

6 Sports Day

How can I organise a sports day?

1 Choose and write. Then match.

jump   throw   run

 1
 2
 3

_____   _____   _____

2 Look and order. Then circle.

CODE CRACKER

1  a   b   2  a   b   3 a    b

 c    c    c

throw / run / jump   throw / run / jump   throw / run / jump

Do you play football?

VOCABULARY

I will learn sport and activity words.

1 Look, choose and write.

> basketball   catch   football   hit   jump   kick   run
> team   throw   table tennis   volleyball   watch

1 _____ 2 _____ 3 _____ 4 _____

5 _____ 6 _____ 7 _____ 8 _____

9 _____ 10 _____ 11 _____ 12 _____

EXTRA VOCABULARY

2 🎧 030 Look, listen and say. Then match.

cricket

badminton

ice hockey

I can use sports and activity words.

75

Language lab 1

GRAMMAR 1: I'M JUMPING

I will talk about actions using I'm ...ing.

1 Do the crossword.

Down ↓   Across →

I'm ...

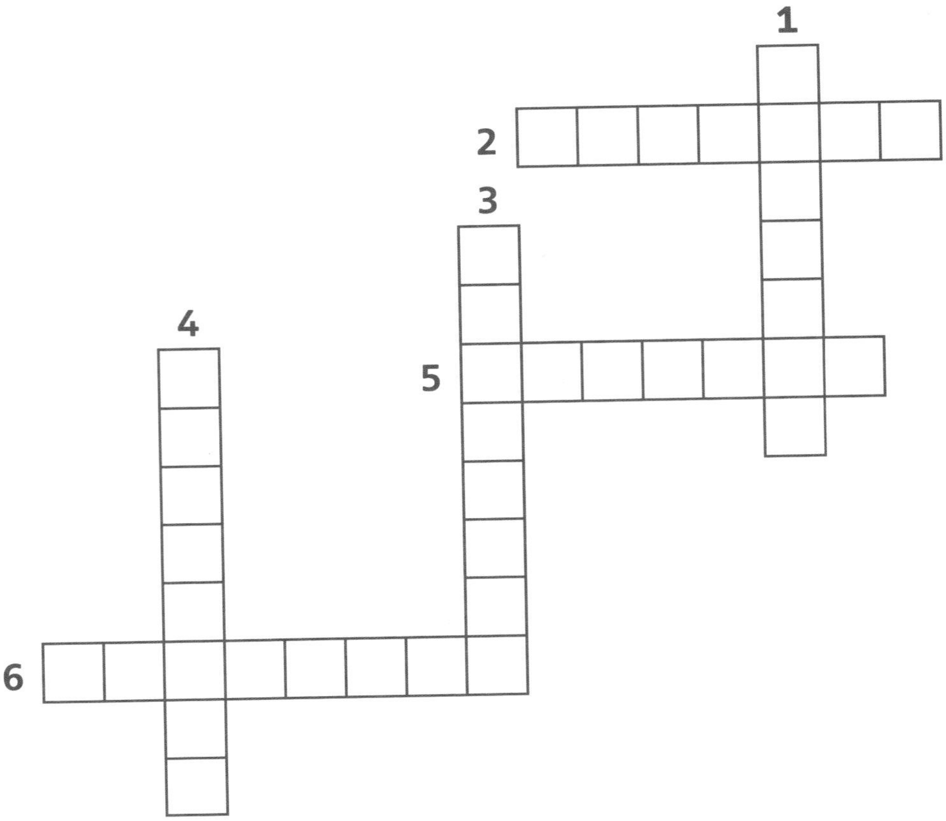

2 Write questions with Are you ...? Then listen and circle the correct answer.

1 (run) _____   Yes, I am. / No, I'm not.

2 (climb) _____   Yes, I am. / No, I'm not.

3 (swim) _____   Yes, I am. / No, I'm not.

4 (jump) _____   Yes, I am. / No, I'm not.

3 Write for you.

1 Are you reading now? _____

2 Are you running now? _____

Yes, I am.   No, I'm not.

4 Order and write.

1 volleyball playing . I'm

_____

2 tennis Are ? playing you table

_____

3 a I'm . ball kicking

_____

5 Tick ☑ two sports and cross ☒ two sports. Then ask and answer with a partner.

playing	watching	
		football
		volleyball
		table tennis
		basketball

I'm playing football. Are you playing football?

No, I'm not. I'm watching football.

6 Now write about you and your partner.

football

1 I'm _____ .

You're _____ .

table tennis

3 _____

_____

volleyball

2 _____

_____

basketball

4 _____

_____

I can   talk about actions using I'm ...ing.

77

Story lab

READING

I will read a story about a game of football.

GOAL!

1 Look, choose and complete.

Are   not   running

Run, Anna! _____ you running, Leo?

I'm _____ !

I'm _____ running. I'm jumping!

River   score

Goal!

The _____ is _____ School 1, Castle School 1.

Kick   kicking

_____ , Leo!

I'm _____ !

coming   leg

Ow! My _____ !

I'm _____ , Leo!

2 Read and circle.

ANOTHER GREAT GAME!

There are three / two teams; Green School and Castle School.

Leo is playing for Castle School. Leo is kicking / catching the ball.

Goal for Castle School!

Now a girl on the Green School team is / are running and kicking and … goal!

Now Leo is running and swimming / jumping … goal for Castle School.

Well done, Green School and Castle School. Bad / Great game!

3 Read again and write the score.

Green School	Castle School

4 Make a football game. Play with a partner.

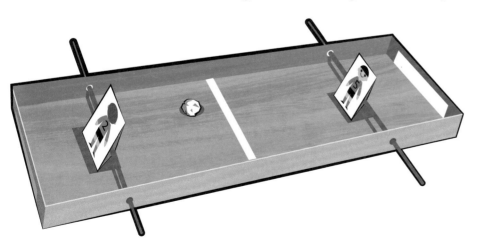

Goal!

5 What happens next? page 126

I can read a story about a game of football.

I will learn the **th** sounds.

1 🎧032 Write th. Then sing the song.

SONG ♫ TIME

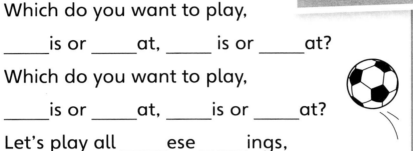

Which do you want to play,

_____is or _____at, _____ is or _____at?

Which do you want to play,

_____is or _____at, _____is or _____at?

Let's play all _____ese _____ings,

Let's play all _____ese _____ings toge_____er!

2 🎧033 Listen and number. Then say.

a   I can throw three things. ☐

b   I can throw thirteen things. ☐

c   I can throw these things. ☐

3 Write th and match.

1   _____ree •

2   _____irteen •

3   _____ank •

4   _____row •

• **13**   • **3**

I can   use the **th** sounds.

Experiment lab

MATHS: MEASURING

I will learn about measuring things in sports.

1 🎧 034 Listen, choose and write.

court   field   net

 **1**    **2**   **3**

1   a table tennis _____

2   a football _____

3   a basketball _____

2 🎧 035 Listen and say.

20 30 40 50 60 70 80 90 100

twenty   thirty   forty
fifty   sixty   seventy
eighty   ninety
one hundred

EXPERIMENT TIME

Report

1 How far can you blow?
Colour the graph.

MATHS ZONE

centimetres

100
90
80
70
60
50
40
30
20
10
0

2 Now write the
numbers in words.

I can blow the pencil
_____ centimetres.

I can blow the tissue
_____ centimetres.

I can blow the straw
_____ centimetres.

 **I know** about measuring things in sports.

Language lab 2

GRAMMAR 2: CAN YOU ...?

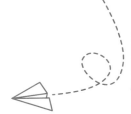

I will ask and answer about actions using **Can you ...?**

1 Read and match.

1 climb	2 play	3 catch	4 ride	5 jump	6 count
a bike	one metre	table tennis	a tree	to 100	two balls

2 Complete the table and write Yes, I can. or No, I can't. for you.

Can you ...?		Yes, I can. / No, I can't.
play table tennis?		_____
_____		_____
_____		_____
_____		_____

3 Complete four questions with your own ideas. Then ask a partner and circle.

1 Can you play _____ ? Yes, I can. / No, I can't.

2 Can you draw a _____ ? Yes, I can. / No, I can't.

3 Can you _____ ? Yes, I can. / No, I can't.

4 _____ ? Yes, I can. / No, I can't.

I can ask and answer about actions using Can you ...?

Can you juggle?
COMMUNICATION

I will talk about activities with my friends.

1 🎧 036 **Listen and number.**

**2 Play the *Can you ...?* game with a partner.
Ask, try, then tick ☑ or cross ☒ .**

Can you ...	Me	My partner
draw a cat with a hat?	☐	☐
jump and count to 20?	☐	☐
write three food words?	☐	☐
dance and say 'five funny fish'?	☐	☐

I can talk about activities with my friends.

1 Tick ☑ or cross ☒ and write in the table for your Sports Day.

Games	✓ / ✗	Who is playing?
Table tennis		
Juggling		
Yoga		
Hula hoop		
Basketball		
Balloon volleyball		
Sack race		

2 Choose, circle and write for you.

> juggling   playing balloon volleyball   playing football   watching

At our Sports Day ...

1   I'm / I'm not / My friend is / My friend isn't _____ .

2   I'm / I'm not / My friend is / My friend isn't _____ .

3   I'm / I'm not / My friend is / My friend isn't _____ .

4   I'm / I'm not / My friend is / My friend isn't _____ .

I can organise a Sports Day.

3 Draw and write.

My favourite game is table tennis.

I can hit the ball.

My favourite game is _____ .

I can _____ .

4 Read, choose and complete.

> not   can   jumping   can't   dancing   tennis
> Are   playing   running   Can   Yes   Are

1 _____ you _____ football?

No, I'm _____ . I'm watching!

2 Are you _____ ?

_____ , I am! I _____ dance!

3 _____ you play _____ ?

No, I _____ !

4 _____ you _____ in the sack race?

No, I'm not! I'm _____ .

5 Play the *Can you catch and count …?* game with a partner.

20

40

30

Now go to your Progress Chart on page 4.

3 Checkpoint

UNITS 5 AND 6

1 Read and match.

1 Can I have soup, please? •

2 Can you swim? •

3 Would you like a biscuit? •

• Yes, please!

• Of course!

• No, I can't.

2 Draw a path.

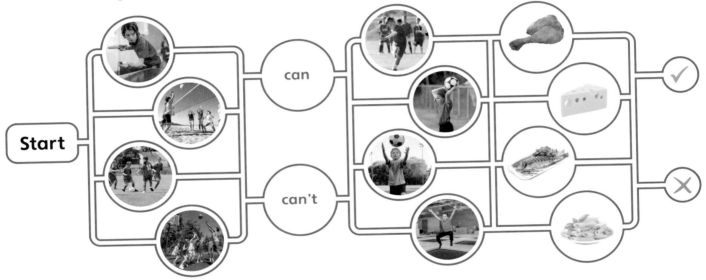

Start

can

can't

3 Look at 2. Circle, complete and draw.

1 I'm playing _____ .

2 I **can** / **can't** _____ .

3 Can I have _____ , please?

4 Compare with your class.

I'm playing volleyball. I can't kick!

I'm playing football. I can kick!

Amazing boat races

CULTURE

1 Find six words. Then choose and complete.

o	s	t	a	n	d	i	h
g	o	n	d	o	l	a	i
n	t	b	u	w	c	h	t
a	d	r	a	g	o	n	t
r	m	c	h	i	n	a	i
i	t	a	l	y	v	x	n
n	g	o	n	d	r	p	g

This is a _____ boat. It's in _____ . The man is _____ a drum.

This is a _____ .
It's in _____ .
You _____ up in the boats.

2 Read and match.

1   The gondola race ●

2   The dragon boat race ●

3   The gondolas are red, ●

4   There are dragon heads ●

● is in June.

● yellow, silver and gold.

● on the dragon boats.

● is in September.

3 Circle, write and draw.

I'm in China / Italy .

I'm watching a _____ race!

I'm eating _____ .

Look at this beautiful boat!

87

7 Our home!

How can I design a dream house?

1 Choose and write. Then match.

1 I wake up in the _____ .

2 I have a shower in the _____ .

3 I make biscuits in the _____ .

bathroom
bedroom
kitchen

2 Look and write. Use the words from 1.

CODE CRACKER

1 I'm going to the _____

2 _____

3 _____

3 Read, listen and match.

This is •   • that we need.

It's a beautiful •   • our house.

It's got everything •   • play and read!

A bedroom, a bathroom, •   • house!

And space to •   • a kitchen.

What's in the bedroom?

VOCABULARY

1 Look and write.

kitchen

2 Read and circle the odd one out.

1 I'm cooking   fish   pasta   library

2 I'm drinking   water   heavy   juice

3 I'm cleaning   football   our car   my table

EXTRA VOCABULARY

3 🎧038 Listen, say and match.

dining room

garage

3
balcony

I can use home and activity words.

Language lab 1

GRAMMAR 1: SHE'S COOKING

I will talk about actions using is / isn't ...ing.

1 Read and match.

1 He is	2 She is	3 It is	4 He is not	5 She is not	6 It is not

It's   It isn't   She isn't   He's   She's   He isn't

2 Complete the table.

Dad   Anna   The owl   Grandad   Leo   Milly the goat   The cat   Mum
The dog   Mrs Hay   My brother   My sister   Miss Kelly   Mr Mud   Grandma

He	She	It
Dad	Anna	The owl

3 Rewrite the sentences using He's, She's or It's.

1 Dad is sleeping. _He's sleeping._____

2 Miss Kelly is singing. _____

3 Leo is reading. _____

4 The owl is waking up. _____

5 Grandma is brushing her teeth. _____

6 My sister is juggling. _____

7 My brother is playing volleyball. _____

4 Look, read and circle.

1 Mum is (cooking) / making a salad .

2 Mum isn't cooking / (making a salad) .

3 Dad is cooking / (making a salad) .

4 Dad isn't (cooking) / making a salad .

5 The cat is drinking / (sleeping) .

6 The cat isn't (drinking) / sleeping .

5 Look, choose and write **is** or **isn't**.

1 The boy _____ drinking.

2 The boy _____ eating.

3 The girl _____ having a shower.

4 The girl _____ looking for a book.

5 The dad _____ eating soup.

6 The dad _____ reading.

7 The cat _____ sleeping.

8 The cat _____ washing its face.

6 What is your teacher doing now? Circle, choose and write.

| cleaning   drawing   reading   sleeping   talking   writing |

1 He's / She's _____ .

2 He / She isn't _____ .

I can talk about actions using is / isn't ...ing .

91

Story lab

READING

I will read a story about everyday activities.

I'm **looking** for Tom!

1 Look, choose and complete.

bathroom big castle going great naughty playing

1 Tom's _____ to the _____ today.

Bye-bye Tom!

2 This is the bedroom.

It's very _____ !
It's _____ !

3 This is the _____ .

Where's Tom?

4 Oh, he's _____ . He's _____ in the bedroom.

2 Read and match.

1 This is the kitchen.

2 This is the bathroom.

3 Where's Tom?

4 I'm looking for Tom.

- I don't know!
- Look! He's cooking!
- He's here.
- There isn't a shower!

3 Read and circle T (True) or F (False).

1 The children are in Castle Town castle.   T / F

2 Tom likes the bedroom.   T / F

3 Leo is looking for Anna.   T / F

4 Tom is playing in the bedroom.   T / F

4 Read and write is or isn't.

The castle _____ very big. There _____
a bathroom. There _____ a shower. Tom _____
playing in the bedroom. He _____ sleeping!

5 Which words are in the story? Tick ☑ or cross ☒.

bedroom	☐	cooking	☐	bathroom	☐	garden	☐
kitchen	☐	big	☐	small	☐	cleaning	☐
sleeping	☐	naughty	☐	funny	☐	great	☐

6 ⚙ Make a castle. Ask and answer with a partner.

Is there a bedroom in your castle?

There are 10 bedrooms!

7 What happens next? ➡ page 127

page 127

I can   read a story about everyday activities.

Phonics lab

I will learn the **wh** and **f** sounds.

1 Write wh. Then listen and say.

1 ____at   2 ____eel   3 ____en   4 ____ich   5 ____ite

2 Write f. Then listen and say.

____ive   ____unny   ____at   ____ish

3 Choose, write and match.

f   wh

1 ____unny •

2 ____eel •

3 ____ite •

4 ____an •

I can use the **wh** and **f** sounds.

Experiment lab

I will learn about good and bad rubbish.

1 Look, choose and write.

fruit   paper   plastic   wood

1    **2**   **3**    **4**    **5**    **6**

_____   _____   _____   _____   _____   _____

2 Now match. Write 1–6.

It IS biodegradable.	
It ISN'T biodegradable.	

EXPERIMENT TIME

Report

1 Choose and write.   paper bag   plastic bag   soil   water

1    **2**    **3**    **4**

_____   _____   _____   _____

2 Circle, choose and write.   good rubbish   bad rubbish

1   The plastic bag is / isn't biodegradable. Plastic is _____ .

2   The paper bag is / isn't biodegradable. Paper is _____ .

I know about good and bad rubbish.

Language lab 2

GRAMMAR 2: IT'S HER HOUSE.

1 Find, write and circle.

Carol

Ricky

1 ___Whose___ book is it? It's his / (her) book. It's ___Carol's book___ .

2 _____ car is it? It's his / her car. It's _____ .

3 _____ ruler is it? It's his / her ruler. It's _____ .

4 _____ aeroplane is it? It's his / her aeroplane. It's _____ .

2 Whose toys are they? Do the maths.

MATHS ZONE

50 pence   25 pence   40 pence   90 pence   65 pence   80 pence

Tina	My toys are …		Mark	My toys are …
1	100 – 60 = _____		4	100 – 35 = _____
2	5 x 5 = _____		5	10 x 5 = _____
3	25 + 15 + 40 = _____		6	45 + 45 = _____

I can talk about objects and belongings using 's.

Look at my photos!

COMMUNICATION

I will talk about family activities in my house.

1 🎧 041 Read, listen and circle a or b. Then role-play.

1 a This is our kitchen.   b This is our house.

2 a I'm reading.   b I'm doing my homework.

3 a Is that your mum?   b Is that my mum?

4 a Is your dad talking?   b Is your dad cooking?

5 a He's cooking.   b He's talking to my sister.

6 a Great photo.   b Great kitchen.

Is that your mum?

Yes!

2 Draw and write for your family.

Where are they?

_____

Who's this?

1 _____

2 _____

What is he/she doing?

1 _____

2 _____

3 🔵 Now talk about your pictures with a partner.

This is our living room.

Is that your dad?

No, it's my brother!

Is he eating?

No, he's playing a game!

I can talk about family activities in my house.

Design a dream house

Project report

1 Tick ☑ or cross ☒ and write for your dream house.

	How many?	big	small
bedroom			
bathroom			
living room			
kitchen			
garden			
_____			

2 Draw one room in your dream house. Then write.

Which room is it? _____

Whose room is it? _____

3 What are you doing in your dream house? Choose or write your own ideas.

> eating   painting   playing
> sleeping   swimming

> bedroom   living room
> swimming pool   garden

I'm _____ in the _____ .

My mum / dad / brother / sister / friend is _____ in the _____ .

I can design a dream house.

4 Read and write answers.

My name's Simon. It's Saturday and I'm at home with my family. Mum is in the living room. She's reading. Dad is in the bathroom. He isn't having a shower. He's brushing his teeth. My sister, Julia, is in her bedroom. She isn't sleeping. She's painting a rainbow. My brother, Mark, is playing football in the garden. I'm in the kitchen. I'm not eating. I'm writing.

1 Where's Simon's mum? She's in the _____ .

2 Where's Simon's dad? He's in the _____ .

3 Where's Julia? She's _____ .

4 Where's Mark? _____

5 Where's Simon? _____

5 Whose is it? Read again and match.

- It's Dad's.
- It's Julia's.
- It's Simon's.
- It's Mark's.
- It's Mum's.

6 Play the *Who am I?* game with a partner.

I'm in the bathroom! I'm not having a shower!

You're Simon's dad!

Now go to your Progress Chart on page 4.

8 Our world

How can I create a nature scrapbook?

1 Look, choose and write.

bridge   down   up

_____

_____

_____

2 Choose and write.

CODE CRACKER

bat   bird   owl   porcupine   river   rock   snake   sun

I look up!	I look down!
I can see a / an / the …	
_____ _____	_____ _____
_____ _____	_____ _____

3 🎧 042 Choose and complete. Then listen and check.

The trees are g_____ .

The sky is b_____ .

I'm having fun in the trees with y_____ !

Climb up, climb u_____ .

Climb up, climb very high!

Don't look d_____ .

Look, look at the sky!

The t_____ are high.

The s_____ is, too.

I'm having f_____ in the trees with y_____ !

Are you up in a tree?

VOCABULARY

I will learn nature and direction words.

1 Do the crossword.

bridge   flower   forest   hill   path   rock   tree

Across →

Down ↓

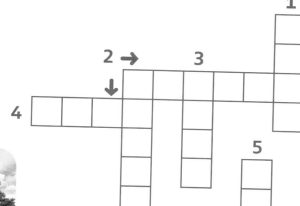

EXTRA VOCABULARY

2 043 Look, listen and say. Then match.

waterfall

lake

island

I can use nature and direction words.

Language lab 1

GRAMMAR 1: WALK / DON'T WALK

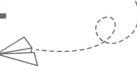

I will understand and give instructions.

1 Choose and write.

Don't turn left   Don't turn right   Go straight on   Turn left   Turn right

1  **2**  **3**  **4**  **5**

1 _____   2 _____   3 _____

4 _____   5 _____

2 Follow, find and write.

CODE CRACKER

a farm
b school
c shop
d museum
e library
f playground
g swimming pool
h café

Where are you?

1 Go straight on for five squares. _____

2 Go straight on for seven squares, turn left, go straight on for three squares. _____

3 Go straight on for six squares, turn right, go straight on for two squares. _____

4 Go straight on for eight squares, turn right, go straight on for four squares. _____

You are here

3 **How do you get there? Look at** 2. **Circle and write.**

Go straight on Turn

1 The swimming pool

Go _____ for ⬜ squares.
Turn (left / right) . _____
straight on for ⬜ squares.

2 The museum

Go _____ for ⬜ squares.
_____ left / right . _____
straight on for ⬜ squares.

4 Now add more letters to 2 and tell a partner where to go.

Go straight on for … squares.
Turn … . Where are you?

5 Make a stop sign. Then play the *Dance! Stop!* game.

Dance, jump, turn left, dance … STOP!

STOP

I can understand and give instructions.

Story lab

I will read a story about helping others.

1 Look, choose and complete.

bridge forest that This

1 Wow! _____ is an amazing _____ !

Look at _____ _____ !

bridge going Me on too

2 I'm _____ the _____ !

I'm _____ up!

_____ _____ !

castle fantastic farm our schoo[l]

3 It's _____ here!

I can see _____ _____ !

And the _____ and the _____

2 Which words are in the story? Tick ☑ or cross ☒.

goat	☐	house	☐
down	☐	fantastic	☐
forest	☐	up	☐
trampoline	☐	amazing	☐
cake	☐	farm	☐

3 Order and write.

1 Milly! , done Well

_____

2 now down ! Come

_____

3 ! the Get trampoline

_____

4 jump with Let's Milly!

_____

4 Read and tick ☑.

Who ...	The children	Milly	Miss Kelly	Mrs Hay	Mr Mud
likes the forest?					
climbs up?					
climbs down?					
has got a lot of food?					
jumps down?					
jumps on the trampoline?					
helps Milly?					

5 Look, read and circle.

Milly / Mrs Hay has got a lot of food.
She's got bread / rice , apples / cheese
and biscuits / ice cream . The children are
very happy / sad .

6 What happens next? ➡ page 128

I can read a story about helping others.

Phonics lab

> I will learn the **s**, **sh**, **j** and **ch** sounds.

1 Say the words. Then circle.

 **1**  **2**  **3**  **4**

1 j   ch   s   sh

2 sh   ch   s   j

3 s   j   ch   sh

4 s   sh   j   ch

2 Write ch, sh, s or j and match.

1 ____icken ☐

2 ____op ☐

3 ____ell ☐

4 ____eese ☐

5 ____uice ☐

6 ____oup ☐

a Mini Market

OPEN   **b**   **d**   **e**   **f**

SOUP   **c**

3 Choose and write. Then listen and chant.

jump (x4)   shoes   Sun

I've got new _____ !

I can _____ !

_____ , _____ , _____

in the _____ !

I can use the **s**, **sh**, **j** and **ch** sounds.

Experiment lab

SCIENCE: LANDFORMS

I will learn about landforms.

1 Circle T (True) or F (False).

1   Our world has got water and land.   T / F

2   Land is made of rocks.   T / F

3   Rocks are always the same colour.   T / F

4   Hills and mountains are made of water.   T / F

5   Tectonic plates are rocks.   T / F

6   Tectonic plates are above the Earth.   T / F

EXPERIMENT TIME

Report

1 Answer for you. Write and circle.

1   How many towels have you got?   _____

2   Do you push the towels?   Yes / No

3   Do the towels go up?   Yes / No

2 Draw your towel mountains.
Then choose for you and write.

> don't look like   don't move
> look like   move

I think the towels _____ mountains.

Tectonic plates _____ .

Language lab 2

GRAMMAR 2: ON, IN, UNDER, NEXT TO, BEHIND …

1 Choose and write.

> behind   in   next to   on   under

1 _____   2 _____   3 _____   4 _____   5 _____

2 Where are they? Do the maths. Then choose and write.

MATHS ZONE

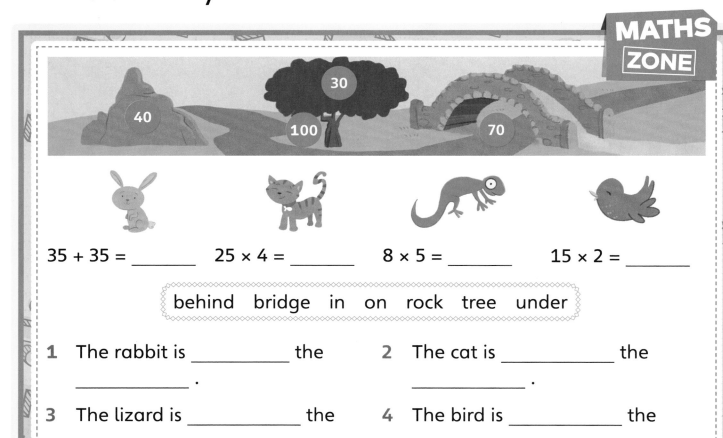

$35 + 35 =$ _____ $25 \times 4 =$ _____ $8 \times 5 =$ _____ $15 \times 2 =$ _____

> behind   bridge   in   on   rock   tree   under

1   The rabbit is _____ the _____ .

2   The cat is _____ the _____ .

3   The lizard is _____ the _____ .

4   The bird is _____ the _____ .

I can use words to describe where things are.

Draw a forest!

COMMUNICATION

I will understand and give instructions to play a game.

1 🎧 045 **Listen, draw and match.**

CODE **CRACKER**

2 💬 **Work with a partner. Choose and tell them where to draw four more things.**

(a river) (a fish) (a donkey) (a girl) (a boy)

(a bridge) (a hill) (a path)

Draw a donkey!

Okay. Where?

Next to the big tree.

3 💬 **Now play the *True or false* game with your partner.**

In my picture, the fish is in the small tree!

False!

Make a nature scrapbook

Project report

1 Write and tick ☑ or cross ☒ for your scrapbook.

	What's it called?	A photo	A drawing	A real thing
flower				
tree				
bird				
animal				
_____				

2 Read and circle for you.

I like / don't like taking photos.

I like / don't like drawing animals / birds / flowers .

I like / don't like learning the names of trees.

3 Draw your favourite thing.
Then write and circle.

It's a sunflower.

It's yellow.

It's near my school.

It's beautiful!

What is it? _____

What colour is it? _____

Where is it? _____

I think it's fantastic / beautiful /
amazing / wonderful .

I can make a nature scrapbook.

4 Circle eight words. Then find and underline them in 5.

bridgejumpingdownuptreehillrivermountain

5 Look, read and match.

My name's Alicia. I'm having fun with my family and friends.

1 Look at me! I'm in a tree! I'm climbing up the tree. ☐

2 I'm walking on a bridge with my family. The bridge is an old tree! It's above the river. ☐

3 I'm jumping with my friends. We're on a hill. Jump, jump, jump! ☐

4 Look at my sister! She's going down a mountain! She's very happy! ☐

6 Read and complete to describe pictures in 5. Use words from 4.

a The _____ is above the _____ .

b Alicia and her friends are _____ on a _____ .

c Alicia is climbing _____ the _____ .

d Alicia's sister is going _____ a _____ .

Now go to your Progress Chart on page 4.

4 Checkpoint

1 Find the words and complete.

u c j i e   n u r t   e e t r   n g i m k a

k n g i n d i r   f l t e   x t e n

1   Is he drinking _____ ? No, he's _____ water.

2   Is she _____ a cake? Yes, she is.

3   Don't _____ right! Turn _____ .

4   .Is the bird _____ to the tree? No, it's above the _____ .

2 Draw a path.

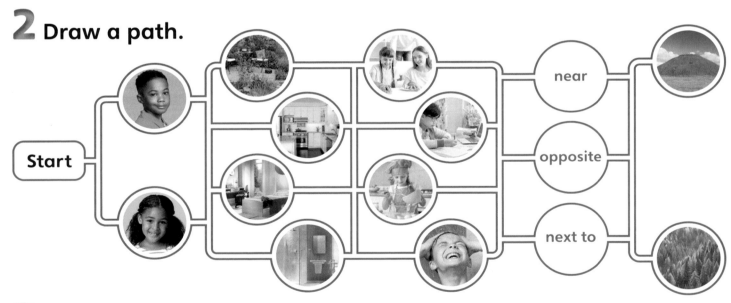

Start

near

opposite

next to

3 Look at 2. Circle and write. Then ask and answer.

1   Who is it? It's _____ .

2   Where is he / she ? He's / She's _____ .

3   What's he / she doing? He's / She's _____ .

4   Where is the house? It's _____ .

Beautiful gardens

1 Choose, complete and match.

beautiful   city   garden
giants   rock   walls

1   Some people grow flowers on roofs and _____ . ☐

2   This _____ is in England. ☐

3   There are _____ in this garden. ☐

4   This garden is in a big _____ , Singapore. ☐

5   Plants make cities look _____ . ☐

6   The giants are made of _____ . ☐

2 Read and tick ☑ T (True) or F (False).

T   F

1   The giants have got hair made of leaves and grass. ☐ ☐

2   The Lost Gardens of Heligan are not old. ☐ ☐

3   There are no gardens in Singapore. ☐ ☐

4   Plants, trees and flowers make oxygen. ☐ ☐

Welcome!

A story about introducing myself at school

Nice to meet you!

Who's _____ ?

I've got a _____ ... Anna!

How _____ is she?

She's _____ .

Oh, _____ , Milly! Nice to _____ you!

Good _____ , children! My _____ is Miss Kelly. I'm your _____ . We're Class 2A.

_____ morning, Miss Kelly!

Draw your teacher.

My favourite character:

_____

My favourite story picture: ☐

☆ ☆ ☆

Yes, I'm Anna and I'm _____ .

Do you _____ cars and books?

Yes, I _____ ! I like _____ , too!

_____ ! My name's _____ . I'm eight. I like frogs and lizards and _____ !

What's _____ name?

I'm _____ .

_____ old are you?

_____ eight. I like books and cars!

Who's _____ ?

It's _____ ! It's Milly the _____ !

Unit 1

A story about a town

A special day

Draw a birthday cake for Castle Town.

Look! A _____ !

Wow! _____ town is _____ today!

We're here, _____ Kelly!

Oh, _____ ! _____ , Anna!

_____ ! I can't _____ !

_____ , Anna!
I _____ hear music!

_____ happening, Leo?

I _____ know!

My favourite character:

_____

My favourite story picture: ☐

☆ ☆ ☆

I like the _____ !

It's _____ and _____ !

We've got a big _____ !

Happy _____ , Castle _____ !

_____ you!

_____ welcome!

Good _____ , Miss Kelly!

Good morning! Come into school. Where are _____ and _____ ?

Unit 2

A story about farm animals

Do goats dance?

_____ , Mrs Hay. What's happening?

I _____ know!

This is a _____ . Goats _____ grass and _____ .

Miss Kelly ... cows _____ and goats _____ !

_____ , Tom!

Look, _____ and _____ . This is a _____ . It eats grass.

Draw your favourite animal.

My favourite character:

_____

My favourite story picture: ☐

_____ goats _____ , Miss Kelly?

No, Tom! They _____ dance!

On the _____ !

To Mrs Hay's _____ , please!

_____ cows _____ , Miss Kelly?

No, Tom. They _____ sing. They say ' _____ '!

They _____ the music! They like _____ _____ !

Unit 3

A story about «something Anna finds»

«Cuckoo!»

Cuckoo! Cuckoo! _____ !

_____ !

It's _____ . It's dirty. It's made of _____ .

A cuckoo _____ ! It's _____ and beautiful!

It's his! It's _____ !

Yes, it's _____ !

_____ plants! Can you dig here _____ , Anna?

Yes, of course, Mr _____ !

Draw a cuckoo clock.

My favourite character:

_____

My favourite story picture: ☐

There's a _____ !
There's a _____ !
Whose is it?

It's _____ cuckoo clock! It's mine!

I've got a _____ .
Yes ... the small _____ key!

Mr Mud, there is something _____ here! _____ is it?

What _____ it look like?

What's the _____ , Mr Mud?

_____ o'clock ... no ... _____ ... no ...

Cuckoo! Cuckoo! Cuckoo!

Unit 4

A story about a painting competition

Who is this?

The _____ cup goes to … _____ !

Congratulations, Mr Mud!

Who is this, Mrs Hay?

It's my _____ .

Is she _____ ? She looks angry.

Er … no … she's _____ .

I've got my _____ .

Great! I've got _____ and crayons.

It's a rainbow! _____ , you are very _____ !

I've got a _____ !

Draw a rainbow.

My favourite character:
_____

My favourite story picture: ☐

This is very _____ , Mr Mud!

Thank you. Milly is sometimes _____ but she is _____ .

OK, finish _____ pictures now, _____ !

_____ is this, Tom?

It's my cousin. He's _____ naughty and _____ happy!

_____ _____ Milly!

Unit 5

Come over and play!

Look at the story on pages 80 and 81 of your Pupil's Book. What happens next? Tick ☑ an ending. Then add your own idea.

Unit 6

Look at the story on pages 94 and 95 of your Pupil's Book.
What happens next? Tick ☑ an ending. Then add your own idea.

Milly, you're on Castle School team now!

Run, Milly! Yes … goal!

I'm playing table tennis with Milly!

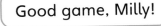

Good game, Milly!

Milly's sleeping!

Good night, Milly!

You can add your own ideas!

Unit 7

I'm looking for Tom!

Look at the story on pages 112 and 113 of your Pupil's Book. What happens next? Tick ☑ an ending. Then add your own idea.

Where's Tom now?

He's in the castle bathroom! He's washing his face!

Where's Leo?

He's in the castle bedroom. He's jumping on the bed!

Where's Miss Kelly?

She's in the castle kitchen. She's making a cake!

You can add your own ideas!

Unit 8

Up and down!

Look at the story on pages 126 and 127 in your Pupil's Book. What happens next? Tick ☑ an ending. Then add your own idea.

Let's climb a tree!

Yes, let's go up, up, up!

Let's eat the ice cream!

Yes, strawberry and chocolate ice cream!

Let's go home!

Good idea! We're tired and happy.

You can add your own ideas!